British History

CASTLES & KNIGHTS

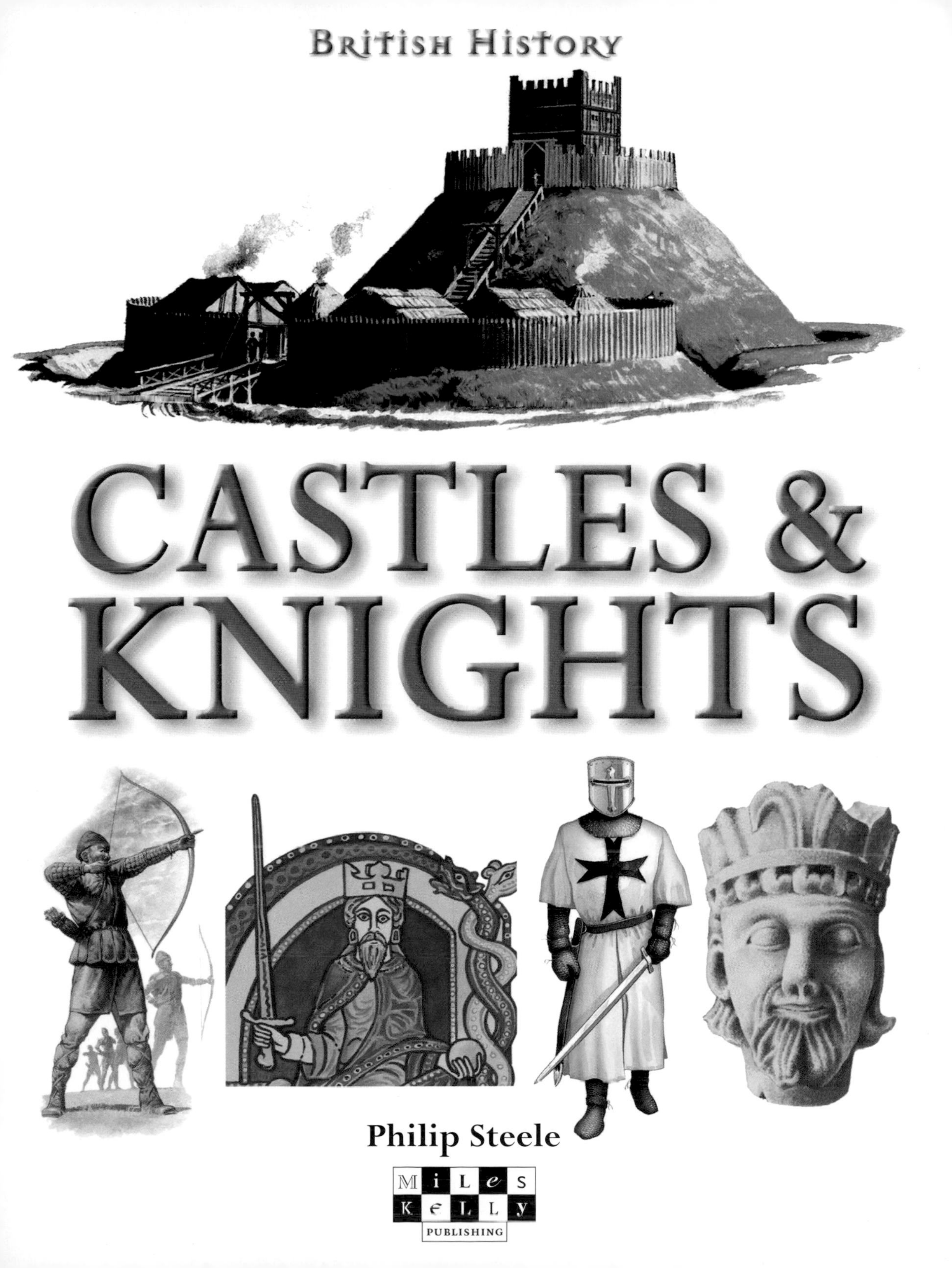
BRITISH HISTORY
CASTLES &
KNIGHTS
Philip Steele
Miles Kelly
PUBLISHING

First published in 2002 by Miles Kelly Publishing Ltd,
Bardfield Centre, Great Bardfield, Essex, CM7 4SL

ISBN 1-84236-142-2

2 4 6 8 10 9 7 5 3 1

Some material in this book can also be found
in the *Encyclopedia of British History*
Project Manager: Kate Miles
Art Director: Clare Sleven
Artwork Commissioning: Janice Bracken & Lesley Cartlidge
Picture Research: Ruth Boardman
Referencing: Liberty Newton
Assistant: Lisa Clayden
Repro: DPI

Contact us by email: info@mileskelly.net
Website: www.mileskelly.net

Printed in Hong Kong

CONTENTS

THE WORLD AT A GLANCE 8-9

HASTINGS 1066 10-11

THE MAILED FIST 12-13

THE FEUDAL SYSTEM 14-15

IS MIGHT RIGHT? 16-17

THE ANGEVIN EMPIRE 18-19

THE CRUSADES 20-21

KNIGHTS IN ARMOUR 22-23

THE AGE OF CASTLES 24-25

TO THE GLORY OF GOD 26-27

THE WELSH PRINCES 28-29

SCOTTISH FREEDOM 30-31

THE PALE AND BEYOND 32-33

A MEDIEVAL TOWN 34-35

THE HARD LIFE 36-37

THE HUNDRED YEARS' WAR 38-39

THE WELSH RISE UP 40-41

WARS OF THE ROSES 42-43

A MEDIEVAL CASTLE 44-45

INDEX 46-47

ACKNOWLEDGEMENTS 48

INTRODUCTION

Massive stone castles still tower over the landscapes of the British Isles, guarding lonely mountain passes, valleys and coasts and towering over market towns that today are peaceful and quiet. They are a reminder us of the violent years of the high Middle Ages.

Knights were often away for long periods of time fighting in the crusades.

Ladies sitting in their beautiful finery watch their knights compete in jousting tournaments.

Castle-building was brought to the islands by the Normans, the descendants of Vikings who had settled in France. They conquered England in 1066, and were soon carving out lordships on the Welsh borders, settling in southern Scotland and invading Ireland. The most important Norman soldiers were armed horsemen, and these 'knights' soon became powerful members of society.

The Middle Ages were troubled times, when the common people suffered greatly from hunger and disease and were forced to toil on the land. Kings ruled their lands with force and were often prepared to use it even against members of their own family. Challenges to royal rule from other sections of society came in the form of violent uprisings, the limiting of royal power through laws and the development of parliaments. England, Wales and Scotland began to emerge as united countries.

Castles were often under threat of seige and needed a ready army of soldiers to defend against attack.

Noble families sought power through marriage alliances, and royal marriages brought the English kings and queens vast new territories in France. England was the growing power, almost perpetually at war with the French, the Welsh and Scots. It was also trying to bring Ireland under its control. Wales suffered defeat in 1283, but England was at last forced to recognize Scottish independence in 1328.

All the countries of the British Isles saw themselves as part of Christendom, a Europe united by the Christian faith and headed by the Pope in Rome. Christian knights repeatedly went to war against Islamic armies in the Near East and in Spain.

Christian monks and nuns were engaged in teaching and caring for the sick, and in copying out beautiful, illustrated texts by hand. New inventions entered Europe from Asia, along with imported silks and spices. The first universities were founded. Languages of the British Isles, such as English, Welsh, Scots and Irish Gaelic, began to take on forms we can recognize today, and be used more widely, alongside Latin and Norman French.

Poetry and literature flourished, and many of the texts glorified the life of the knights and their ladies and the code of honour they were supposed to follow. This ideal of 'chivalry' was never more than a dream, but it was one which would inspire many future generations in the British Isles.

The castle kitchens were always busy preparing food for the lords and ladies being entertained upstairs.

CASTLES AND KNIGHTS

AD1066–1509

THE WORLD AT A GLANCE

ELSEWHERE IN EUROPE

1220
King Frederick II of Sicily and Germany becomes Holy Roman Emperor

1226
Louis IX (St Louis) comes to the throne in France

1237
Mongol armies invade East and Central Europe (to 1241)

1378
A split in the Roman Church, with one Pope in Rome and another in Avignon, France

1453
Turks capture Constantinople (Istanbul). End of the Byzantine empire

1462
Lorenzo de Medici rules over splendid court at Florence, Italy

1480
Ivan the Great, first Tsar of Russia, expels the Mongols and unites his country

1492
Christians finally reconquer all of Moslem Spain, rule of Ferdinand and Isabella

ASIA

1096
European Crusaders attack Moslems in the Near East and found Christian kingdoms

1170
The Hindu Srivijaya kingdom rules Java, Southeast Asia

1190
Temujin (Genghis Khan) starts to create the Mongol empire

1192
Yoritomo Minamoto becomes first Shogun (military dictator) in Japan

1206
The Islamic Sultanate rules in Delhi, India

1271
Mongol ruler Kublai Khan becomes the emperor of China

1368
Ming emperors rule China, capital at Nanjing

1405
Death of Timur the Lame (or Tamberlaine), Tatar ruler of a vast Asian empire

AFRICA

1200
The rise of the state of Mali in West Africa

1200
Rise of Hausa city-states in northern Nigeria and Kanem-Bornu in Lake Chad region

1250
Rise of the Benin empire in southern Nigerian forests

1250
High stone enclosures built at Great Zimbabwe, in southeast Africa

1300
Founding of the Kongo kingdom in southern Central Africa

1400
Chinese, Arab and Indian traders along East Africa's Swahili Coast

1400
Fine heads made from bronze in the Benin empire

1450
Height of Songhai power in southern Sahara, university at Timbuktu

"The peasant toils, the king rules – and God is in His heaven..."

Llywelyn Fawr

NORTH AMERICA

1100
Thule culture of the American Arctic, based on whaling

1150
The Anasazi people settle Mesa Verde in the southwest

1170
Collapse of Toltec rule in Mexico, period of wars and strife

1300
The Maya people return to power in Mexico, with capital at Mayapán

1345
Aztecs build the great city of Teotihuacan on the modern site of Mexico City

1428
The Aztec empire expands and becomes very powerful

1492
Christopher Columbus, in the service of Spain, lands in the Caribbean

1493
The Spanish settle on the Caribbean island of Hispaniola

SOUTH AMERICA

1100
The city of Cuzco, Peru, is founded by the first Inca emperor

1370
The Chimú empire expands in northern Peru

1450
The founding of the Inca town of Machu Picchu, high in the Andes

1470
The Incas conquer the Chimú empire

1492
The Incas conquer northern Chile

1493
The Treaty of Tordesillas. Spain and Portugal divide up the Americas.

1498
The Inca empire is at its greatest extent under ruler Wayna Qapaq

1500
The Portuguese claim Brazil

OCEANIA

1100
Increased farming and irrigation begins on the Hawaiian islands

1200
Powerful chiefdoms grow up in Polynesia

1200
The Tu'i Tonga dynasty rules the Tongan Islands and part of Samoa

1200
Large numbers of stone platforms and houses built in the Society Islands

1250
Funeral of the Melanesian ruler Roy Mata on the island of Retoka

1300
Giant moa is hunted to extinction in New Zealand, increase in agriculture

1350
Classic Maori period begins on New Zealand, large fortresses

1400s
Malay fishermen camp on shores of northern Australia

✤ **1064** Harold swears to support William of Normandy

✤ **1066** Harold II chosen as King of England

✤ **1066** King Harald III of Norway defeated at Stamford Bridge

✤ **1066** Norman invasion. Harold II defeated at Battle of Hastings

✤ **1067** William I starts to build the Tower of London

HASTINGS 1066

WHO WERE THE NORMANS?

The Anglo-Saxon kings were not the only ones who attempted buy off the Vikings. In AD 911 Charles 'the Simple', King of France, offered a Viking warlord called Rollo part of northern France in a desperate bid to win peace. It became called Normandy ('land of the Northmen'). Rollo became a duke and married Giselle, a French princess. Like their Viking ancestors, Norman warlords stormed their way around Europe. They invaded the Italian island of Sicily in 1060.

IN the summer of 1066 a large fleet assembled along the French coast. Its commander was William, Duke of Normandy. Ships wallowed at anchor in choppy seas, waiting for the northerly wind to turn. Norman lords galloped to and fro on horseback. Carts trundled along the beach loaded with spears, swords, arrows and axes, iron helmets, shields and coats of mail. This would be the last major invasion of England in the Middle Ages.

Archers
The bow used by the Normans was about 1.5 metres long and was drawn to the chest. It was said that a Norman arrow pierced King Harold's eye and killed him.

Wooden weapons
Bows were made of elm, but arrows of ash. The flights were made from goose feathers.

The Battle of Hastings remains the most famous event in English history. Its shockwaves were felt right across the British Isles.

CLAIMS FOR THE THRONE

Harold of Wessex was the son of a powerful Anglo-Saxon earl called Godwin. In January 1066 the Witan named Harold as King of England, but their decision was challenged at once. Edward the Ætheling, nephew of Edward the Confessor, claimed the throne. So did Harold's own brother, Tostig. A third claimant was King Harald III of Norway, known as 'Hardraade', 'the Ruthless'. The fourth was William of Normandy. William swore that in 1064 Harold had made a solemn vow to support the Norman claim.

RULERS OF ENGLAND
House of Normandy

✤ William I 'the Conqueror'	1066–1087
✤ William II 'Rufus'	1087–1100
✤ Henry I 'Beauclerk'	1100–1135
✤ Stephen	1135–1154

1068 Norman conquest of northern and western England

1069 Anglo-Saxon uprising, led by Edward the Ætheling

1070 Rebellion in East Anglia by Hereward 'the Wake'

1085 William I orders compilation of the Domesday Book

1087 War with France, William I dies after he falls from horse

One battle too many

Harold II's troops were waiting for the Normans when word came that Harald III of Norway had joined forces with Tostig. Harold marched northwards at speed. He defeated and killed them both at Stamford Bridge, near York. Just three days later, Norman troops landed in Sussex. Harold had to march his exhausted army south again. On 14 October 1066, the two great armies clashed at Senlac Hill, near Hastings. All day, wave after wave of Normans broke against the Anglo-Saxon shields. Harold's men stood firm but, scenting victory, they broke rank too soon. The victory belonged to William – 'the Conqueror'.

Shield The long kite-shaped shield was developed by the Norman cavalry

Helmet The iron, cone-shaped helmet was worn over a hood of mail, called a coif.

Coats of mail Norman warriors protected themselves with a mail shirt worn over a tunic.

This tapestry of wool on a linen backing has a 70-metre long 'strip' format, which tells the story of the Noman invasion of England. It can still be seen today in Bayeux, Normandy.

The Domesday Book

Exactly 19 years after his coronation, William I announced that all the lands in England south of the rivers Ribble and Tees (and excluding the cities of London and Winchester) were to be registered in a great book. From 1086 onwards, royal officials travelled from one estate to another. They wrote down the details of buildings, land and resources, so that they could be taxed.

The Tower of London was added to over the ages. It played a central role in English history, with many famous prisoners being locked up in its dungeons.

The conquest

On Christmas Day 1066, William I was crowned king in Westminster Abbey. Within months of his coronation, William ordered the building of a new fortification by the River Thames, in London. Its great keep, or stronghold, was the White Tower. This became the centre of the Tower of London.

Within two years most of England was under his control. Revolts led by Edward the Ætheling and an Anglo-Saxon lord called Hereward the Wake ('the Watchful') were crushed.

1066 The Norman Channel Islands come under the English crown

1072 William I of England leads army into Scotland

1092 Normans build castle at Pembroke in South Wales

1094 'Marcher' Lordships established in the Welsh borders

1094 Norman invasion of North Wales

THE MAILED FIST

THE Norman kings of England and their successors wanted to be recognized as overlords of all the British Isles. Their fleets sailed north and their armies were soon battling with the Scots. Norman warlords were given territories on the Welsh borders (the 'Marches'), and stormed into North and South Wales. Within a hundred years, their great castles of stone could be seen in Ireland, too.

Dermot, the Irish ruler of Leinster, needed the support of Strongbow (right). In return he offered him the hand of his daughter, Aoife, and succession to the throne of Leinster

Braided hair
Norman ladies often wore their hair in plaits. Heads were sometimes covered with a short veil, secured by a circlet of silver or gold.

A cloak
A long woollen cloak was worn for warmth, fastened across the front by a cord.

The girdle
A cord or jewelled belt was worn around the waist.

A flowing dress
A long-sleeved shift was covered by a long tunic called a bliaut, which was laced at the side.

A Norman lady

THE NORMANS IN SCOTLAND

After repeated Scottish invasions of his new kingdom, William I marched into Lothian at the head of a large army in 1071, but he made peace with Malcolm Canmore at Abernethy. In 1092 the Normans took Cumbria from the Scots, but a full-scale invasion of Scotland never occurred. Norman settlers did arrive, bringing their ways to the Lowlands and to the Scottish court. Later Scottish kings, including Robert Bruce and the Stewarts, were of Norman descent.

Supplies
Weapons and equipment had to be carried with the troops. Food and grain could be seized by force along the way.

1097 Normans defeat Donald III of Scotland

1100 William II of England is killed, possibly murdered, in the New Forest

1106 Henry I of England defeats and imprisons his brother Robert in Normandy

1166 Dermot MacMurrough of Leinster invites Normans into Ireland

1170 Normans invade from Baginbun, Wexford

Wales and the marches

The Norman kings did not intend to rule Wales directly, but they wished to control it. As early as 1067 William I gave land on the borders to William Fitzosbern, Roger Montgomery and Hugh d'Avranches. These 'Marcher Lords' were a law to themselves. They launched savage raids into North Wales in the 1080s. By the 1090s Norman warlords were gaining control of large areas of South and West Wales. They met fierce resistance, but this was a period when the Welsh kingdoms were at war with each other. The Normans were defeated in 1096 at Gelli Carnant, Gwent, but they kept their foothold in Wales.

GWENLLIAN GOES TO WAR

Gwenllian was the daughter of Gruffudd ap Cynan, ruler of Gwynedd in North Wales. She married another Grufudd, son of Rhys ap Tewdwr, ruler of Deheubarth. In 1136 her husband went to meet her father, to plan a rising against the Normans in South Wales. While he was away, Gwenllian led a warrior band to storm Kidwelly castle. They were beaten back and defeated by Maurice de Londres. Gwenllian was killed in the attack.

Horse power The Normans used highly mobile forces to control their conquests.

Metal in motion The mounted knight was the key to Norman success.

Strongbow's Ireland

In Ireland, warring between provincial kings gave a chance for descendants of the Normans to invade. In 1166 Dermot MacMurrough, King of Leinster, appealed to Henry II of England for help. He had lost his lands in the wars between Ireland's provincial kings. Henry authorised Norman lords to carry on this fight independently.

In 1169 Richard fitz Gilbert de Clare, Earl of Pembroke, agreed to help Dermot in return for land. De Clare, half Norman and half Welsh, was known as 'Strongbow'. His invasion of Ireland was successful – too much so for Henry II, who was jealous of Strongbow's new-found power. The English king and his army arrived in Ireland in 1171.

The Norman invasion did not stop at the borders of England.

✤ **1086**
Population of 2 million in area surveyed by the Domesday Book

✤ **1086**
Domesday Book records over 2 million hectares of land as cultivated

✤ **1191**
First record of windmills being used for grinding wheat

✤ **1200s**
Rapid growth of towns and cities

✤ **1300s**
Feudal system begins to be replaced by a money-based economy

THE FEUDAL SYSTEM

THE division of society into classes of serfs, free men, nobles and rulers had started earlier in the Middle Ages. The Normans were the first to enforce this 'feudal' system rigidly. The king was at the top, ruling by the will of God. He parcelled out land to his lords in return for their support. The land was worked by free men and serfs (or 'villeins'), who provided the nobles with food and served in their armies. In return, the poor were, in theory at least, protected by their lord.

Kings of the Middle Ages held extreme power over their subjects. Every royal document was marked with a personal badge called a seal, pressed into soft wax. This one belonged to Henry I of England.

Oaths of loyalty

The feudal system was a series of two-way contracts, reinforced by oaths of loyalty. The loyalty was not to a nation, but to a noble or royal family. A lord could even insist that 'his' people take up arms against their own countrymen. The feudal system crossed national borders. Europe's ruling classes were allied with each other, rather than with the peasants who worked for them. If a king from one royal family married the princess of another, the lands they ruled might be joined together, regardless of public opinion or geography.

Field use
One field might be for oats and another for wheat. The third might lie 'fallow' (uncultivated) and be grazed by cattle. Field use changed from year to year so that the goodness in the soil was not all used up.

The feudal economy was based on land and services rather than money. It only worked if people stayed on the land. Villeins were not allowed to leave their village and were forced to work on their lord's estates.

⚜ 1300s Rise of a middle class made up of merchants and craft producers

⚜ 1300s Cloth production moves out of towns, water power needed for fulling

⚜ 1300s Spinning wheels introduced into the British Isles

⚜ c1330 The *Luttrell Psalter* includes illustrations of everyday English life

⚜ 1349 Ordinance of Labourers tries to limit English wages

WOMEN IN THE MIDDLE AGES

In the medieval (Middle Ages) period, most women in Europe had few rights. Strict vows bound together man and wife, just as society was bound by oaths of feudal loyalty. It was the men who held real power and wealth. Despite this, many women were strong characters and became widely respected in their own right. There were powerful queens and noblewomen, abbesses and nuns, scholars and poets, and able working women in every village. In the later Middle Ages, poets began to sing the praises of women, but in a very idealized way.

Women may have been honoured in medieval poetry but in reality had hard lives. Many died in childbirth.

RICH AND POOR

The Norman lords who had supported William I during the invasion of England profited hugely. They were rather like the lottery winners of today, only their new-found wealth was based on land rather than money. This created problems for kings that followed, for there were now many very powerful lords who could challenge their rule. At the other end of the scale were the villeins. They had to labour on the lord's land for, say, three days a week. They also had to pay taxes and supply farm produce to the lord. The Church too demanded one-tenth (a 'tithe') of their harvested crops.

Windmill
Windmills, originally an Asian invention, were first built in Britain during the 1190s. They were mounted on an upright post, and could be turned so that the sails caught the wind. They were used for grinding grain into flour.

Harrow
A harrow was a spiked frame used for preparing the soil ready for the seeds to be scattered by the sower.

IS MIGHT RIGHT?

IN the days of William the Conqueror, life was short and violent. The road to kingship was not through election or consent. It was often through murder and battle. Even the laws reflected the belief that 'might is right'. A legal dispute might be settled by an official fight – 'trial by combat' – or by making the accused grasp a red hot bar of iron – 'trial by ordeal'. God, it was believed, would punish the guilty and protect the innocent.

Armed might invades the peace of Canterbury Cathedral in 1170. Four knights have burst in to murder English archbishop Thomas Becket while he prays.

A KING'S NIGHTMARES

In 1100, William II of England was killed in a hunting accident in the New Forest. Or was it murder? Nobody knew for sure. Six years later his successor, Henry I, imprisoned his own brother for 28 years. A series of pictures drawn in the 1140s shows Henry I haunted by royal nightmares. Haughty bishops, armed knights and angry peasants all protest by his bedside.

THE FIGHTING EMPRESS

When Henry I's son was drowned at sea in 1120, he named his daughter Matilda as his heir. She lived in Germany at that time, for she had been betrothed (engaged to be married) at the age of just seven to the Emperor Henry V. She had married him in 1114, aged twelve. Widowed in 1125, Matilda soon remarried another very powerful but younger man, Geoffrey of Anjou. She fought desperately for the English throne until 1148.

Matilda flees from Oxford. She was unpopular with the English people. At one time she captured Stephen, but was never crowned queen.

A TIME OF TERROR

Henry I did manage to keep order in the land, but after his death in 1135, there was chaos. Before his chosen heir, Matilda, arrived back in England, the throne was seized by Stephen, a grandson of William I. There followed 13 years of war between the two. It was a terrible period for the common people, as lord fought lord and armies looted the land.

TRIAL BY JURY

A fairer legal system was brought in by Henry II of England during the 1100s. Punishments for crimes were still often brutal, but now courts were held around the country in the king's name. Juries were called to decide guilt or innocence. In those days, juries were not independent members of the public but people who may have known the accused or witnessed the crime.

Bishops and barons

The Roman Church was very powerful. Popes believed that as God's representatives they had the right to control European politics. Quarrels between kings and the Church became common. In 1170 supporters of Henry II of England murdered Thomas Becket, the Archbishop of Canterbury. Another challenge to royal power came from barons (powerful nobles). In 1215 English barons forced King John to agree to recognize their legal rights. The agreement was known as *Magna Carta* ('the great charter'). The barons did not need protection, but at least the law was now recognized as more important than the word of kings and queens.

King John was a weak ruler. In 1215, at Runnymede, near the River Thames, he caved in to the demands of his rebel barons and signed the Magna Carta.

A SUMMONS TO PARLIAMENT

Magna Carta may have been one of the first moves towards social justice, but its immediate effect was to make the warring barons even more powerful. When Henry III of England came to the throne in 1216, he was only a child. In 1258 he was forced to hand over power to the barons. Their leader was Simon de Montfort, Earl of Leicester and brother-in-law of the king. He imprisoned Henry III at Lewes, Sussex, in 1264. The next year de Montfort called a great council, or 'parliament'. Each county sent a knight and each town sent a burgess (leading citizen). De Montfort was killed in 1265, but parliaments were again summoned by later kings. By 1352 parliment had two sections or 'chambers'. The House of Lords was for the nobles and the bishops, while the House of Commons was for knights and burgesses.

THE ANGEVIN EMPIRE

ALTHOUGH Matilda failed to win the throne of England, her son was crowned King Henry II in 1154. His royal line is sometimes called Plantagenet, named after the sprig of broom (in Old French, *plante genêt*) that his father Geoffrey wore in his cap. Henry II ruled over a huge area of western Europe called the Angevin (Anjou) empire.

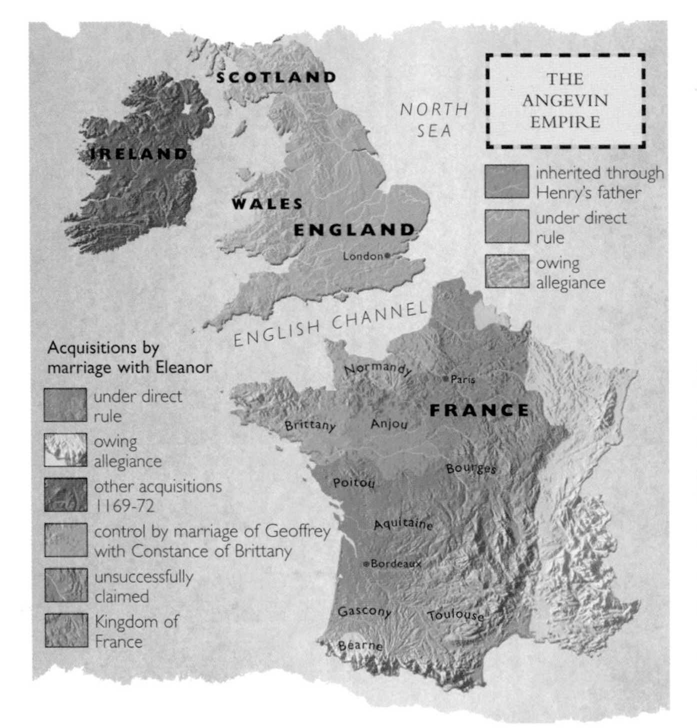

WHICH LANGUAGE?

The English spoken today began to take shape in medieval England. It grew out of several languages. The court used French, while scholars and the Church used Latin. Most ordinary people spoke dialects of English. Other languages spoken in the British Isles at this time included Cornish, Welsh, Scots Gaelic, Irish and Norse.

ROYAL LANDS

Henry II's lands stretched from the sunny vineyards of Bordeaux in southwest France, to the rainy Scottish borders. He had inherited Anjou from his father and gained Poitou, Aquitaine and Gascony on marrying Eleanor of Aquitaine. Henry also claimed to be overlord of Brittany, Wales, Scotland and Ireland.

RULERS OF ENGLAND

House of Anjou (Plantagenet)

✤ Henry II 'Curtmantle'	1154-1189
✤ Richard I 'Cœur de Lion'	1189-1199
✤ John 'Lackland'	1199-1216
✤ Henry III	1216-1272
✤ Edward I 'Longshanks'	1272-1307
✤ Edward II	1307-1327
✤ Edward III 'of Windsor'	1327-1377
✤ Richard II	1377-1399

THE EMPIRE UNRAVELS

Henry II of England was energetic and fiery-tempered. He was a very able ruler, but he quarrelled bitterly with his wife and with his sons. They rebelled against him and the great empire began to break up. Royal power lessened under Stephen and John, but the struggle to control France would continue for hundreds of years.

ELEANOR OF AQUITAINE

Eleanor of Aquitaine was one of the most remarkable women in medieval Europe. She was born in about 1122. She became Duchess of Aquitaine in 1135, when she married the heir to the French throne. He was crowned Louis VII two years later. Eleanor was unconventional and beautiful. She and a troop of women, dressed as classical warriors, joined the Second Crusade (one of the wars between Christians and Moslems in the Near East). After her marriage was annulled (cancelled) in 1152, Eleanor married young Henry of Anjou, who became King Henry II of England. Their love soon turned sour and when Henry was unfaithful she supported his sons in rebellion against him. She was imprisoned from 1174 until the death of Henry in 1189. She died in 1204.

The lute was widely played in western Europe in the Middle Ages. Musicians performed at court and poets and singers travelled from one castle to another.

Eleanor's court in Poitou attracted poets, musicians and scholars from all over Europe.

SCHOLARS AND INVENTORS

Under Plantagenet rule in England, few people could read or write. Some children were taught in church schools or were tutored by monks or nuns. University students may have been studying at Oxford as early as 1167, and Cambridge University was founded in 1215. One scholar who studied at Oxford and Paris was Roger Bacon (c1214-1292). He was a scientist who predicted the use of flying machines and telescopes. At this time all sorts of exciting new inventions were arriving in Britain from abroad, including gunpowder, clocks and spectacles.

FOOD FOR A ROYAL BANQUET

England's medieval language divide has survived in the kitchen today. English-speakers raised 'sheep', but the French-speaking nobles who ate them called them '*moutons*'. 'Mutton' later became used for the cooked meat.

Medieval feasts or banquets included huge pies and tarts, jellies, fish such as eels and lampreys, roast goose or swan and venison. Dishes were served with great ceremony.

boar's head

✤ AD632
Death of Muhammad, founder of Islam, in Arabia

✤ 1075
Moslem Turks capture the holy city of Jerusalem

✤ 1095
Pope Urban II calls for a holy war or 'Crusade'

✤ 1096
The First Crusade leaves Europe for the Holy Land

✤ 1099
Crusaders capture Jerusalem, massacre 40,000 Jews and Moslems

THE CRUSADES

In 1075 the city of Jerusalem was captured from its Christian rulers by Turkish Moslems. Twenty years later, Pope Urban II appealed to all Christian knights to launch a holy war, or Crusade. Its aim was to recapture Jerusalem and the 'Holy Land'. The First Crusade began in 1096 and Jerusalem was taken after three long years.

Moslem lands stretched from Spain through North Africa to Southwest Asia. The Christian lands of Europe were known as Christendom. The Christian lands of the Near East were called Outremer ('overseas').

Jews, Christians, Moslems

By now, most of Europe was Christian. The Moors (Moslem Berbers and Arabs) had conquered much of Spain, but were under constant attack by Christian armies from the north. There were communities of Jews in many parts of Europe, too. Their ancestors had been expelled from Jerusalem by the Romans in AD 70. In Moorish Spain, Moslems, Christians and Jews lived peaceably together. However in most of Christendom, religious hatred against Moslems and Jews ran rife. Jews were persecuted terribly in England and in 1290 they were expelled by Edward I.

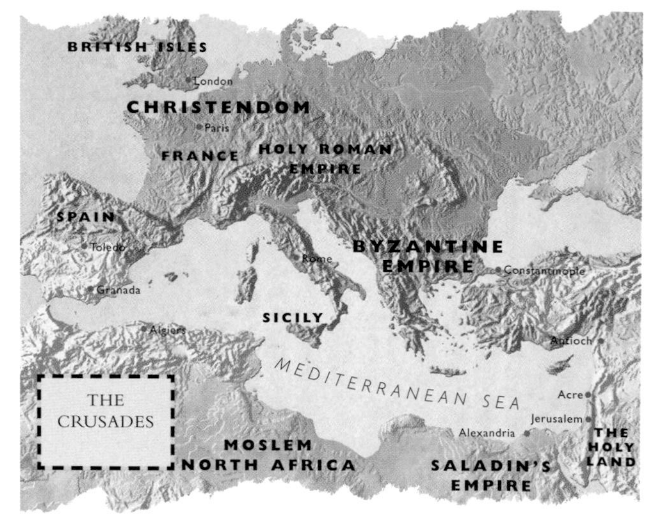

RICHARD THE LION HEART

One of the most famous English kings, Richard I spent only 10 months of his reign in England and probably spoke only French. In 1189 he became King of England. In the following year he joined the Third Crusade, at first with King Philippe Auguste of France. In 1191 he captured the city of Acre. Richard's exploits brought him fame and the nickname *Cœur de Lion* ('Lion Heart'). Journeying home, Richard was shipwrecked and forced to cross the lands of his enemy, Duke Leopold of Austria. He was captured and handed over to Emperor Henry VI. A huge sum ('a ransom') had to be paid for his release and it was the English people who had to find the money. Richard was killed fighting against France in 1199.

Richard I, son of Henry I and Eleanor of Aquitaine, spent most of his reign at war.

The Crusader
Crusaders were armed with swords, lances, axes and maces. Their armour varied over the years. Chain mail gave way to solid plate armour.

Religious wars

There were several further Crusades between 1096 and 1270. These shameful wars poisoned relations between Christianity and Islam into modern times. Religious motives soon gave way to looting and land-grabbing. Moslems were not the only enemy. In 1204, Crusaders turned aside to sack the Christian city of Constantinople. In 1208 a Crusade was launched against Christians in southern France, who differed from Rome in their beliefs. German Crusaders invaded Poland and the Baltic lands in the 1200s.

Saracen weapons
The Saracens had swords of the finest steel, spears and round shields. Archers fired arrows from small bows while riding.

Saracen armour
Moslem troops either wore tunics which were padded or sewn with metal plates, or coats of mail.

Fighting in the dry heat and dust of the Near East, when weighed down with armour and weapons, was often an ordeal. Although the Crusades were meant to be 'holy' wars, the citizens of besieged towns were often slaughtered without mercy. The Crusades left a bitterness between Christianity and Islam that still affects the politics of Southwest Asia today.

Crusaders and Saracens

Crusaders came from all over Europe, including the British Isles. Some joined international 'orders', such as the Knights of St John (founded in 1099), or the Knights Templar (1119). The Moslem soldiers of the 'Holy Land' were called Saracens and included Arabs, Turks and Kurds. Their most famous leader was Salah-ed-din Yussuf ('Saladin',1137-1193). He earned the respect of many Crusaders. Contact with Arab civilization opened the eyes of many Europeans to the wider world.

1066 Norman knights wear long tunic of mail ('hauberk')

1099 The Order of the Knights of St John is founded

1119 The Order of Knights Templar is founded

1200s Horses protected with padded or mail coats called trappers

1292 Statute of Arms lays down rules for English tournaments

KNIGHTS IN ARMOUR

Knights might be away at the wars for years on end. Castles and households were often managed by their ladies.

In the 700s, a simple invention had reached Europe from Asia – stirrups. They supported the legs of a horseback rider and made it possible for mounted soldiers to charge the enemy really hard, without falling. By Norman times, horse soldiers called knights had become the most important part of most armies. Even lords and kings had to learn how to be good knights. In the 1100s and 1200s, almost every battlefield shook to the thundering hooves of great war-horses leading a cavalry charge.

A fine display
Fancy crests, plumes and scarves were worn at tournaments to impress the spectators.

Jousting helmet
The 'great helm' worn for tournaments was padded with straw.

Coats-of-arms
In tournaments and battles even the horses displayed coats-of-arms.

HERALDRY

In a tournament or a battle, it was hard to tell one armoured knight from another. Knights began to use personal badges or emblems, which were displayed on surcoats (tunics worn over armour), on shields and standards. These emblems were passed down from one generation of a family to another. They became known as coats-of-arms and can still be seen carved on castle stones or coloured in the stained glass of old churches. The rules for drawing up coats-of-arms are known as heraldry.

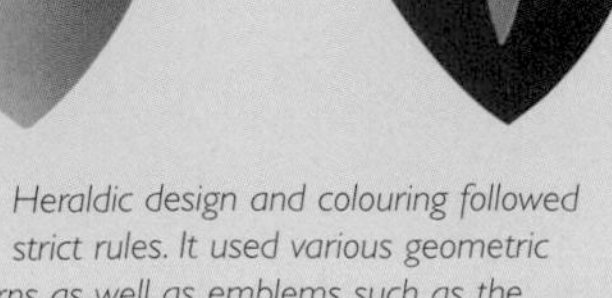

Heraldic design and colouring followed strict rules. It used various geometric patterns as well as emblems such as the fleur-de-lys ('lily flower', above right).

THE AGE OF CHIVALRY

In the high Middle Ages, knights developed a code of behaviour, called 'chivalry'. It was based on Christian virtues. A knight vowed to protect the weak, honour women, keep his word and respect his enemies. These ideas were admired by many later generations, but they were only ever an ideal. Battles may have had strict rules, but they were still brutal affairs. Respect was certainly not extended to peasants or to enemy foot soldiers, who were slaughtered without mercy.

1300s
'Coat of plates' – armoured plates stitched to tunics

1330s
Solid breastplate encases the upper part of the body

1334
Edward III of England founds knightly Order of the Garter

1400s
Full plate armour covers whole body

c1490
James IIII of Scotland founds knightly Order of the Thistle

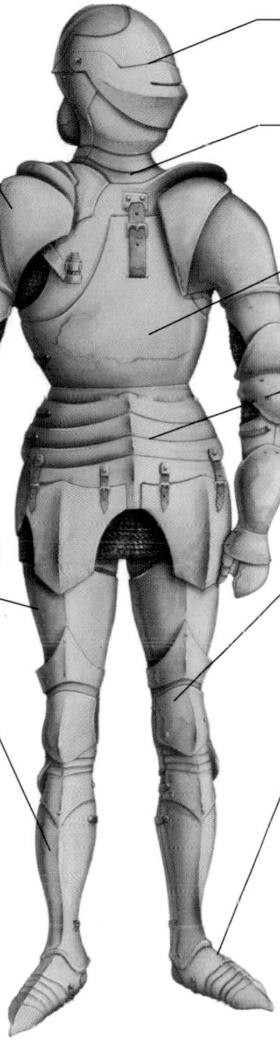

Helmets
Now protected the whole face as well as the skull.

Pauldrons
Shielded the shoulders from heavy blows.

Gorgets
Were plates which prevented the throat being stabbed.

Breastplates
Covered the ribs.

Cowters
Covered the elbows.

Skirts
Plate strips protected the waist.

Gauntlets
Were jointed, armoured gloves.

Cuisses
Protected the thighs.

Poleyns
Protected the kneecaps.

Greaves
Protected the shins and lower leg.

Sabatons
Were pointed, armoured shoes.

By the 1400s, plate armour encased the knight's whole body.

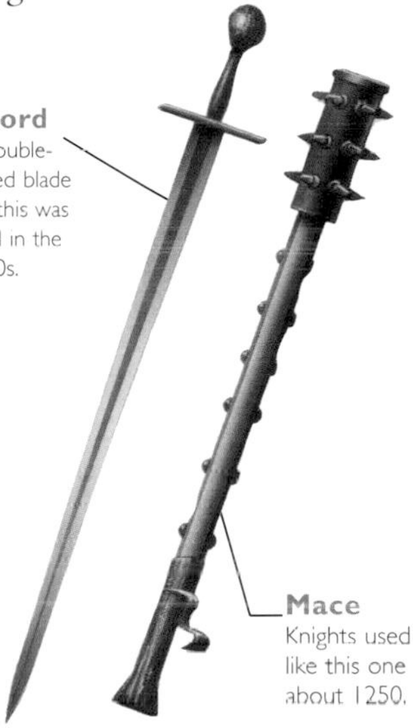

Weapons used in hand-to-hand fighting included clubs (called 'maces') and all kinds of swords and daggers.

Becoming a knight

Young boys started to learn how to be a knight at about the age of seven, when they were sent to serve as a page in a castle. They were taught to fight, ride and use weapons. At about 14 they became an esquire, or assistant to a knight, and could go into battle. At about 21, or earlier if they showed great courage, esquires would be made full knights.

Sword
A double-edged blade like this was used in the 1300s.

Mace
Knights used clubs like this one after about 1250.

Splendid tournaments

More than 800 years ago, knights turned their military training into a sport. They fought mock battles called *mêlées* and later fought one-to-one, galloping at each other with lances raised. This was called jousting. It was a very violent sport and deaths were common. Grand competitons called tournaments were held, at which young knights sought fame and fortune. Before they took part, they dedicated their fight to a lady of the court.

Two knights clash in a joust. After the 1400s, their horses would be separated by a low wooden fence called a tilt.

✤ cAD 950
Motte-and-bailey castles built in France

✤ 1066
Normans bring castle building to the British Isles

✤ 1100s
Castle defences centred on massive stone towers called keeps

✤ 1180s
Castles built with square wall towers

✤ 1220s
Castles built with round wall towers

THE AGE OF CASTLES

FORTRESSES had been built in Britain in Roman times. After the Normans invaded England in 1066, powerful kings and lords began to build new kinds of fortresses, called castles. Castles served as homes, as well as military bases and centres of government. They were used to control conquered lands and show off the power of their owner. Kings and lords sometimes owned several castles and moved from one to the other during the year.

The first castles were wooden towers called baileys, on top of earthen mounds called mottes. By the 1100s, castles were being built with thick stone walls.

During a siege, armed knights could ride out from 'sally ports' – small gates at the side of the castle – to launch a counter-attack.

LIFE IN A CASTLE

The centre of activity in the castle was the Great Hall. This was where banquets and important meetings were held. In the kitchens, meat sizzled on spits in front of the fire. The bedrooms and the main living room (called a 'solar') were often cold and draughty. Fresh reeds were strewn on the stone floors, as there were no carpets. There were rooms for the servants, guard rooms and stables.

Peasants worked the fields around the castle, supplying it with food. Grain was stored inside the castle walls, in case a siege cut off supplies.

HISTORIC CASTLES

Massive stone castles were built all over England, Wales, Scotland and Ireland. Many of them can still be seen today. Some of them are ruined, but you can still see the holes where joists once supported floors and timbers, or the arrow loops in the walls. Some castles are still in use as museums or private homes.

Edinburgh, Scotland, was fortified in ancient times. Parts of its castle date back to the 1000s.

1290s Concentric castles, built with rings of walls and towers.

1320s The age of gunpowder begins, new threat to castles

1350s Bricks begin to be used in building some castles

1450s Castles start to be replaced by fortified homes and palaces

1600s Last military use of castles in British Isles

KING OF THE CASTLES

Beaumaris castle is on the Isle of Anglesey, in Wales. Work on it began in April 1295 and cost a fortune. It employed no fewer than 2,000 labourers, 200 stonemasons and 400 quarrymen. Beaumaris was the last in a powerful chain of castles built by King Edward I of England to secure his conquest of North Wales. He was the greatest castle builder of his day.

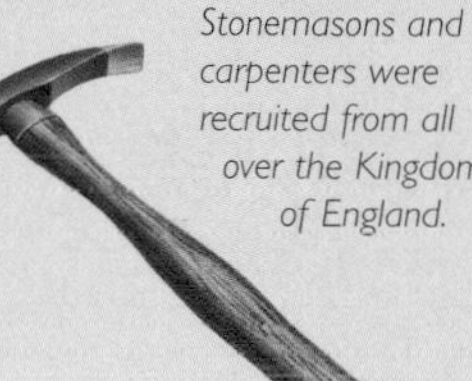

Stonemasons and carpenters were recruited from all over the Kingdom of England.

SIEGE WARFARE

An army trying to attack a castle tried to surround it and cut off its supplies, so that the defenders starved. This was called a siege. Blazing arrows were shot into roof timbers. The walls were pounded with boulders from giant catapults, or undermined with tunnels dug beneath the foundations. More sieges ended by treaty or agreement than by the fall of the castle.

Castles had to be strongly built and heavily defended to withstand attack.

The first cannon were very unreliable, but by the mid-1400s they were used to deadly effect.

Bodiam, Sussex, England, 1386. This castle had holes for firing handguns as well as arrow loops.

TO THE GLORY OF GOD

In later medieval Europe, the Christian faith was part of everday life. It was expressed in the great stone cathedrals and abbeys which were raised all over the British Isles in the Middle Ages. Building styles changed over the years. Some cathedrals had massive, awe-inspiring towers. Others were graceful, with tall spires pointing to heaven. Inside, gold glittered in candle light and coloured ('stained') glass windows glowed like precious gems.

In the Middle Ages, the language of the Roman Church was Latin, which few ordinary people could understand. Most were unable to read either. Stained glass windows were an ideal way of telling worshippers stories from the Bible or the lives of the saints.

Durham Cathedral, towering above the River Wear in the northeast of England, was started by the Normans in 1093. It contains the tombs of St Cuthbert and Bede. During the Middle Ages the bishops of Durham were as warlike as any barons and had great political power.

✤ **1180** St David's Cathedral, Wales, is rebuilt

✤ **1215** Roman Church and Pope at height of power

✤ **1221** Friars enter England for first time

✤ **1250** Westminster Abbey is rebuilt near London

✤ **1380s** Bible first translated into the English language

Monks and nuns lived in monasteries and convents. Some cared for the sick or taught young people. Some travelled from one town to another, living on charity. Religious orders such as the Franciscans ('Grey Friars') or the Dominicans ('Black Friars') were founded in the 1200s.

LETTERS OF GOLD

Before the days of printing, books had to be copied out by hand. The work was often done in monasteries. The pages were made of vellum (animal skin) and decorated with elaborate letter designs and small pictures, called 'illuminations'. Books were such rare and precious objects that they were often chained to the shelf.

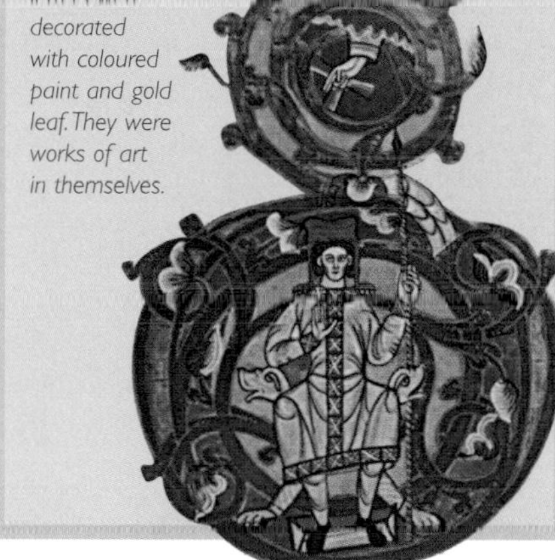

Illuminated letters were decorated with coloured paint and gold leaf. They were works of art in themselves.

MONKS AND NUNS

By about 1215 the Roman Church was at the height of its power and wealth. It was at that time that an Italian monk called Francis of Assisi called for Christians to give up riches and help the poor and the sick. By the 1220s his ideas were being spread through the British Isles by wandering monks, or friars. However many church officials remained greedy and corrupt. They were condemned by an English priest called John Wycliffe, who gained many followers in the 1300s.

MYSTERIES AND MIRACLES

Many people believed in miracles or in the healing power of relics such as saints' bones (which were often fakes). Some Christians became hermits, living alone to meditate. A woman called Julian of Norwich wrote about the meaning of religious visions she had in 1373. At that time a poem called *Piers Plowman* was also written, which celebrated the simple faith of ordinary people. The Bible was not translated into English until the 1380s. One way people could learn about the scriptures was through acting. Religious ('mystery') plays, featuring angels and devils, were performed outside many cathedrals.

CANTERBURY PILGRIMS

Many people went on pilgrimage to holy sites, such as the tomb of Thomas Becket in Canterbury. They prayed for healing or forgiveness of sins. Between 1387 and 1400 a poet called Geoffrey Chaucer wrote about these pilgrims and of the stories they told to pass the time. The *Canterbury Tales* was one of the first and greatest works of English literature.

Amongst Chaucer's pilgrims were a knight, a nun, monks, a miller, a lawyer, a merchant and a doctor – a cross-section of medieval society.

✤ 1063
Death of Gruffudd ap Llywelyn, having briefly united Wales

✤ c1115
Welsh princes start to build their own castles

✤ 1164
Founding of Strata Florida abbey (Ystrad Fflur)

✤ 1165
Owain Gwynedd resists Henry II of England

✤ 1176
Eisteddfod held at Cardigan Castle

THE WELSH PRINCES

WALES in the 1100s and 1200s was a rural land, with few large towns. People farmed and hunted, travelling by narrow tracks through the mountain passes. The princes were guarded by castles built by the Welsh rulers. They also endowed (funded) great monasteries such as Strata Florida (Ystrad Fflur) in the Teifi valley and Llanfaes, on Anglesey. There was a rich tradition of music, and a great gathering of poets (an *eisteddfod*) was held at Cardigan in 1176.

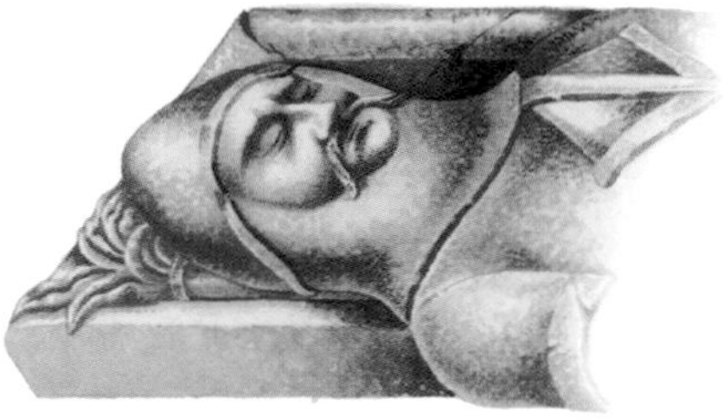

Rhys ap Grufudd ('the Lord Rhys' of Deheubarth) weakened Norman power in South Wales during the chaotic reign of King Stephen in England.

WHO HOLDS POWER?

Under rulers such as Rhys ap Gruffudd in the south and Owain Gwynedd in the north, Norman power in Wales declined. The Marcher Lords still held the borders, however, and the English kings regarded themselves as overlords of the Welsh. The division of Wales into separate kingdoms played into the hands of the English. In 1157 Madog ap Maredudd of Powys helped King Henry II of England invade Wales, in order to weaken his rivals in Gwynedd.

GERALD OF WALES

Gerald de Barri was born in about 1146. His ancestry was part Norman, part Welsh. Gerald became a talented writer in Latin and a great churchman. In 1188 he travelled through Wales with Archbishop Baldwin, and his *Journey Through Wales* and *Description of Wales* give us lively and good-humoured pictures of Wales in the high Middle Ages. He died in 1223 and has gone down in history as Giraldus Cambriensis, or Gerald of Wales.

St David's Cathedral came under the control of Norman bishops in 1115. It was rebuilt in 1182.

1188 Gerald de Barri travels through Wales

1216 Llywelyn Fawr summons parliament at Aberdyfi

1250 Coal being mined at Margam, in South Wales

1267 English recognize Llywelyn ap Gruffudd as Prince of Wales

1283 Llywelyn ap Gruffudd killed in skirmish with English, Cilmeri

RULERS IN WALES

- Gruffudd ap Llywelyn 1039-1063
- Bleddyn ap Cynfyn 1063-75
- Trahaearn ap Caradog 1075-1081
- Gruffudd ap Cynan 1081-1137
- Owain Gwynedd 1137-1170
- Dafydd ap Owain Gwynedd 1170-1194
- Llywelyn 'Fawr' ('the Great') 1194-1240
- Dafydd ap Llywelyn 1240-1246
- Llywelyn ap Gruffudd 1246-1282

Llywelyn II's death near Cilmeri in 1282 marked the end of Welsh independence. He is remembered in Wales as 'The Last Prince'.

THE GREAT LLYWELYN

In 1170 three sons of Owain Gwynedd fought each other at Pentraeth, on Anglesey, for the throne of Gwynedd. Hywel was defeated by Rhodri and Dafydd and the kingdom was divided. By 1194 all Gwynedd had come under the rule of Llywelyn ap Iorwerth, 'the Great'. Llywelyn married Joan or Siwan, daughter of King John of England, but the two rulers later became enemies. Llywelyn was the most powerful ruler in medieval Wales, a strong supporter of the Church and the law.

This stone head is believed to represent Llywelyn Fawr, 'the Great'. He held court at Aberffraw, on Anglesey.

THE LAST PRINCE

Llywelyn was succeeded by his younger son, Dafydd, but he died in the sixth year of his reign. He was to be followed by his nephews Llywelyn and Owain, but the former seized the throne for himself and gained control of all Wales. Llywelyn II ap Gruffudd was recognized as Prince of Wales by the English in 1267. However he would be the last Welsh prince. He quarelled with King Edward I and after long wars, was killed in a skirmish with English troops near Cilmeri. His severed head was displayed in London.

THE CONQUEST

King Edward I of England was now the undisputed ruler of Wales. His castles ringed the land. English criminal laws replaced Welsh ones and the *Statute of Rhuddlan* (1284) divided Wales into counties, along English lines. In 1301 Edward I's son (the later Edward II) was declared Prince of Wales, and ever since then the title has been held by the eldest son of the English monarch.

Conwy castle

✤ **1130s** Norman families gain estates in the Lowlands

✤ **1174** William I of Scotland forced to recognize English king as overlord

✤ **1264** Norwegian invasion defeated at Largs

✤ **1266** Scotland gains Norwegian territories on mainland and Western Isles

✤ **1296** Edward I of England defeats John Balliol at Dunbar

SCOTTISH FREEDOM

In the 1100s, Scotland saw great changes. Norman families gained Scottish lands. Three sons of the great Queen Margaret ruled the country in turn – Edgar, Alexander I and the great David I. Many fine churches and abbeys were built during their reigns, and around them developed prosperous 'burghs' (large towns). Peasants lived in small farming villages called 'touns'.

RULERS OF SCOTLAND

✤ Donald III Bán	1093–1097
✤ Duncan II	1094
✤ Edgar	1097–1107
✤ Alexander I 'the Fierce'	1107–1124
✤ David I 'the Saint'	1124–1153
✤ Malcolm IV 'the Maiden'	1153–1165
✤ William I 'the Lion'	1165–1214
✤ Alexander II	1214–1229
✤ Alexander III	1249–1286
✤ Margaret 'Maid of Norway'	1286–1290
✤ Throne disputed	1290–1292
✤ John (Balliol)	1292–1296
✤ Edward I of England	1296–1306
House of Bruce	
✤ Robert I Bruce	1306–1329
✤ David II	1329–1371
✤ Edward Balliol	1306 & 1333–1336

SCOTLAND STANDS FIRM

In 1174, William I of Scotland was captured by English troops and forced to recognize Henry II as his overlord. It was an act never forgotten by the English – or the Scots. Alexander III, who came to the throne as a boy, had another old enemy to deal with – Norway. The Norwegians invaded in 1263, but were forced to withdraw and finally lost their mainland and island territories.

David I was succeeded by his young son Malcolm IV, who died before he was married.

1297 William Wallace defeats English army at Stirling Bridge

1305 William Wallace captured and executed

1314 English defeated by Robert Bruce at Bannockburn

1328 England recognizes Scotland as independent

1371 Rule of Scotland passes to the Stewarts

Scotland falls

Tragedy now struck the Scots. In 1286 Alexander III fell from his horse and was killed. Four years later his successor, the young girl Margaret of Norway, also died. Who should reign next, was unclear. The Scots turned to Edward I of England for advice. His candidate was John Balliol, a distant descendant of David I. Edward I thought he could control his chosen man, but instead Balliol turned and made an historic alliance with France. Edward I stormed into Scotland in 1296 and defeated Balliol at Dunbar.

Lords of the Isles

In the Highlands and Western Isles, the old Gaelic way of life continued. Here, first loyalty was to the chief of the clan (a group sharing descent from a common ancestor). The lands of Clans Dugall, Donald and Ruairi became known as the Lordship of the Isles. The first Lord of the Isles was John of Islay of Clan Donald, who died in 1387. The Lordship was in constant conflict with the Scottish kingdom and was brought to an end in 1493.

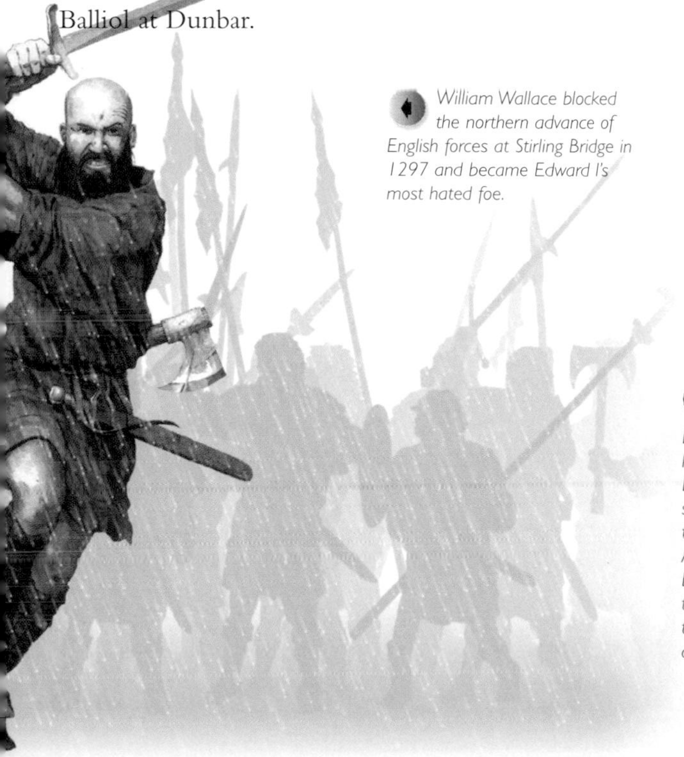

William Wallace blocked the northern advance of English forces at Stirling Bridge in 1297 and became Edward I's most hated foe.

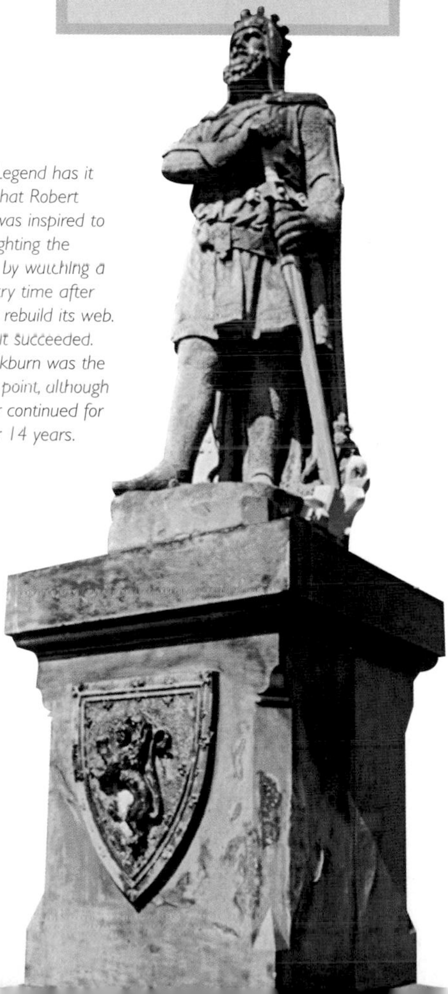

Legend has it that Robert Bruce was inspired to keep fighting the English by watching a spider try time after time to rebuild its web. At last it succeeded. Bannockburn was the turning point, although the war continued for another 14 years.

War of independence

Resistance to English rule was fierce. Its champion was William Wallace, who defeated an English army at Stirling Bridge, but was himself defeated at Falkirk in 1298. Captured in 1305, Wallace was horribly executed in London. Parts of his body were sent to Newcastle, Berwick, Stirling and Perth. The fight was taken up by Robert Bruce (who had stabbed his chief rival, John Comyn, to death). Robert was crowned king by the Scots in 1306. Edward I died in the following year and at Bannockburn, on 24 June 1314, Bruce turned the tide and defeated 20,000 troops of Edward II.

✤ 1175 Treaty of Windsor: Rory O'Connor recognizes Henry II as overlord.

✤ 1210 Irish kings submit to King John of England

✤ 1235 Normans complete conquest of western Ireland

✤ 1257 Irish attack Normans in Sligo and Thomond

✤ 1315 Edward Bruce invades Ireland from Scotland

THE PALE AND BEYOND

THE word 'pale' means fence or enclosure. In medieval Ireland it came to mean the area of the country which was directly controlled by the kings of England. It lay in the east of the country, around Dublin. Within the Pale, English language, laws, fashions, architecture and customs became normal. The Pale was settled not just by English royal officials, but by merchants and labourers too, from across the Irish Sea.

The Breac Maedhóc is a bronze shrine from Drumlane, County Kavan. Its figures show the Gaels of Ireland in the 1100s. The men have long hair and beards and wear long cloaks. The women wear their hair in ringlets.

The area of the Pale varied greatly during the later Middle Ages. By 1464 it included the counties of Dublin, Kildare, Louth and Meath.

THREE WORLDS, ONE LAND

Beyond the Pale, lay the lands of two other groups – the Irish-speaking Gaels and the powerful, independent Norman families who had seized Irish land. Over the years, many of the latter adopted Irish ways. The English kings, however, firmly believed that civilization ended 'beyond the Pale'. This phrase is still sometimes used today to describe unacceptable or uncouth behaviour. From time to time the English attempted to expand their rule by founding colonies beyond the Pale. These were English settlements protected by soldiers.

THE STATUTES OF KILKENNY

From the early days of English rule in Ireland, the official policy was one of separation and apartness. In 1366 the English, under Prince Lionel of Clarence, called a parliament at Kilkenny and passed a wide range of statutes (laws). According to these, English colonists were not allowed to marry into Irish families, or to adopt Irish dress or customs. They were not to speak Irish or use the ancient Irish legal system, known as Brehon Law.

1318 Edward Bruce killed at Battle of Faughart

1320 University founded in Dublin, first in Ireland

1333 English crown loses control of Connaught and Ulster

1366 Statutes of Kilkenny are proclaimed

1394 Richard II of England regains control of Ireland

Barley for the taking

When Henry II of England landed in Ireland in 1171, his chief aim had been to make sure that 'Strongbow' and his adventurers did not set up a Norman kingdom in Ireland to rival his own. As the years went by, the English found another reason for staying in Ireland. The lush, green pastures and fields of ripe barley were a valuable economic resource. Grain from Irish estates could be exported to England or mainland Europe for rich rewards.

Kern and galloglass

Ireland saw wave after wave of English invasion. John came in 1185 as prince and again in 1210 as king. Richard II arrived in 1394–1395 and again in 1399. There were long battles between the old Norman families and amongst the Irish kings. By recognizing the English kings, some Irish royal families managed to survive and even thrive in this changing world. The poor peasants experienced endless warfare. All sides used roving bands of troops who would fight for anyone who paid and fed them. These mercenaries included Norman men-at-arms, Irish footsoldiers called kerns and Scottish adventurers called galloglass, meaning 'foreign warriors'.

These stone carved tombs represent two of Ireland's most powerful families at the close of the Middle Ages. They may be seen in St Canice's Cathedral, Kilkenny. They belong to Piers Butler, Earl of Ossory and Ormond, and his wife Lady Margaret Fitzgerald.

The Rock of Cashel is crowned by splendid buildings from the Middle Ages. Cormac's Chapel dates from 1127–34, while the great cathedral was built about 100 years later.

- **c1170** Major period of town building begins
- **1176** London Bridge is rebuilt in stone
- **1233** Piped water supply to Westminster, near London
- **1250s** Zoo animals including lions in Tower of London
- **c1300** Town building starts to decline

A MEDIEVAL TOWN

Rich merchants began to build with stone. The Jew's House in Lincoln is over 800 years old and has a hall on the first floor.

TOWNS were now beginning to grow quickly. They were noisy, rowdy places and often foul-smelling, too, for there was no proper drainage. Water had to be carried to each house from wells. Carts brought vegetables to market and cattle were herded though the muddy streets. Women tied wooden platforms called pattens to their shoes, to walk through the puddles. Travellers slept huddled together on straw mattreses, in flea-infested inns.

Timber houses
In the Middle Ages, most houses were still built with timber frames and walls of wattle-and-daub. Some of these may still be seen in Britain today.

Open sewers
Waste was thrown into the street and streams were used as open sewers. Birds and dogs scavenged rubbish tips.

WALLS AND CHIMNEYS

Medieval cities were surrounded by walls and at night the gates were locked and barred. Tall wooden-framed houses were crowded together. House fires were common and straw thatch was often banned in favour of slates and tiles, which could not blaze. All cooking fires had to be covered each night – the time of 'curfew' (from the Old French *cuevre-feu*). At first smoke came out through holes in the wall. It was not until the 1400s that chimney pots topped the roofs.

By the 1250s, most of the English population lived within 25 kilometres of a market town. Modern cities that were founded during the Middle Ages include Liverpool, Hull, Leeds, Newcastle upon Tyne, Portsmouth.

OLD LONDON BRIDGE

The first versions of London Bridge were made of wood, and they really did keep falling down, just as it says in the old nursery rhyme. However a 19-arch stone bridge, built between 1176 and 1209, lasted until 1831. On this bridge there were rows of houses and even a chapel. Sometimes the bridge was used for jousting. Traitors' heads were often displayed on the bridge after they had been chopped off.

The wealth of merchants began to compete with that of the nobles and the Church.

MONEY AND MERCHANTS

Merchants became wealthy. In London there were great warehouses owned by the Hanseatic League, a powerful organization which traded right across Germany to the Baltic Sea. Bankers lent money in return for payment of interest. Even kings borrowed from them to pay for their wars. When bankers became richer than kings, it was clear that the old feudal system was breaking down. Craft workers formed trading guilds which controlled the marketing of their wares. Young lads came to stay in the house of the master of their trade and learned how to be a weaver, a tailor or a goldsmith. They were called apprentices.

Shop signs
When most people people couldn't read, shop signs had to be visual. A boot might hang above a cobbler's shop, or a horse-shoe above a smithy. A green bush was the sign of an inn.

Animals to market
Even large cities echoed to the sound of cattle, sheep and geese being driven through the streets to market.

FOOTBALL HOOLIGANS

Apprentices were an unruly lot and often tried to avoid work. They formed gangs on the streets. One of their favourite sports was football. A blown-up pig's bladder served as a ball. There were no rules and the game was played on the street. It was very rough. In 1314 the sport was banned by King Edward II of England.

1314 Weather destroys harvests, major famine

1315 Harvests fail yet again, starvation

1348 Black Death appears in England and Wales

1349 Black Death reaches Scotland, kills one in five

1351 England attempts to freeze workers' wages

THE HARD LIFE

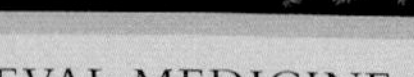

On 14 April 1360 the weather was so foul and bitter that many horseback riders were reported to have died of cold, frozen to death in their saddles. There were few comforts in the Middle Ages. Castles were draughty and stank of sewage from the cesspit or the moat. People rarely bathed and disease was common. Many women never survived childbirth and children often died when small.

MEDIEVAL MEDICINE

Medical knowledge had grown little since the days of the Romans. Surgeons could mend bones and monks grew herbs to make medicines. Some of these cures worked, but many didn't. One common treatment was bleeding – taking blood from the patient.

A leper's clapper

"OUR DAILY BREAD"

While the nobles ate fine wheaten bread, the poor ate crusts of coarse rye. Rye crops were sometimes spoiled by a fungus disease called ergot. People who ate flour made from mouldy rye became sick and saw strange visions. Country people preserved their own food, salting fish and smoking bacon. They ate eggs and caught hares and waterfowl. If the harvests failed and prices rose, then people starved.

Food supply was seasonal and depended on good harvests. Famine was common.

Leprosy was an infectious disease. Lepers had to carry a wooden clapper, to warn people that they were coming along the road.

Sinners and lepers

Natural disasters and illnesses were often believed to be punishments sent by God, because of human sinfulness. One of the most feared diseases was leprosy, which causes lumps, discoloured patches and ulcers to form on the body. Fingers and toes would sometimes become numb and fall off. Sufferers (lepers) were banned from public places and were only allowed to watch church services through a slit in the wall.

Rats and fleas were all too common in medieval towns and cities. The plague was first brought to England by the black rats which used to infest almost every ship.

✤ **1361**
A second outbreak of the plague in Britain

✤ **1369**
A third outbreak of the plague in Britain

✤ **1377**
Poll tax introduced in England

✤ **1381**
Peasants' Revolt in England led by Wat Tyler

✤ **1390**
The plague returns for the fourth time

The Black Death

In August 1348 a new disease appeared at the port of Weymouth, in the southwest of England. It was known as the Pestilence, later as the Black Death. This terrible plague, spread by rats and their fleas, had already devastated Central Asia and Europe. Soon it was raging across England, Wales, Scotland and Ireland. The Black Death took various forms. One poisoned the bloodstream and caused horrid swellings and boils on the body. Another affected the lungs and could be passed on by coughing and sneezing.

In medieval Europe, knowledge of diseases and medicine had not advanced since Roman times. The sick were sometimes cared for by nuns. The Black Death killed many of the carers as well as the patients. Soon, plague victims were being buried in mass graves and there were no priests left to pray for their souls.

A labour shortage

In the years 1347 to 1351, the plague may have killed 75 million people in Asia and Europe. Many villages in the British Isles lost half to two-thirds of their population. In some there were no survivors at all. There was a great shortage of labour, so workers now found that they could demand high wages. The English government passed harsh laws in a desperate bid to keep wages at the same level, in 1349 and 1351.

The Peasants' Revolt

In England after 1377, people had to pay more and more poll taxes (standard payments demanded from all citizens). In 1381 angry peasants from Kent and Essex, led by Wat Tyler and a priest called John Ball, stormed London. Fourteen year old King Richard II rode out to meet the rebels and offered to take up their cause. But Wat Tyler was cut down by the Mayor of London and the rising was savagely suppressed.

Twenty thousand peasants marched on London in 1381. They burnt the palace of John of Gaunt, Duke of Lancaster. They killed the archbishop, captured the Tower of London and set prisoners free.

1337 Edward III of England declares himself King of France

1340 Naval battle off Sluys won by England

1346 English defeat the French at Crécy

1347 English troops capture the French port of Calais

1356 The Black Prince defeats the French at Poitiers

THE HUNDRED YEARS' WAR

THE period we know as the Hundred Years' War was a long drawn out, bloody struggle between England and France. It took place across the muddy battlefields of northern France and Flanders (in what is now Belgium). It was never really one war, but a series of raids, battles, campaigns and treaties. Nor did it last 100 years, but from 1337 until 1453.

Edward 'the Black Prince', was the eldest son of Edward III. His nickname came from the colour of his armour. Edward was a brilliant soldier who made a name for himself when he was only 16, at the Battle of Crécy. In 1356 he won a great victory at Poitiers. He died in 1376.

WHO RULES FRANCE?

King Edward III of England was related to the French royal family and in 1337 he claimed the throne of France as his own. England had fought for its lands in France ever since the days of the Normans and the Angevin empire. What was more, France was now a close ally of Scotland, England's enemy. The result was a war which cost Edward III's subjects dearly. They had to pay for it with taxes, loss of trade – and their lives.

In October 1415, Henry V found his route blocked by a huge French army (foreground) at the village of Agincourt. His 6,000 troops were sick with dysentery and greatly outnumbered, but he won a great victory. The French knights became bogged down in mud, while flight after flight of arrows whistled through the air.

The crossbow was a much more accurate weapon than the ordinary bow.

WEAPONS AND TACTICS

For campaign after campaign, the English raided and plundered northern France. Long columns of battle-weary knights, waggons, footsoldiers and archers trailed across the countryside. Some carried new-fangled handguns, others hauled early cannon. When it came to pitched battles, England's great strength lay in its use of archers, armed with deadly longbows. They could fire up to 12 arrows a minute.

⚜ **1360**
The Peace of Brétigny between England and France

⚜ **1415**
Henry V of England wins the battle of Agincourt

⚜ **1420**
The *Treaty of Troyes*. Henry V becomes heir to the French throne

⚜ **1431**
The English burn Joan of Arc as a witch at Rouen

⚜ **1453**
English defeat at Castillon, end of the 100 Years' War

The game of chess

The English were not alone in their attacks on the French kings. At times they were allied with the Bretons of the northwest, at times with powerful barons from Burgundy, in the east. At first the English achieved some great victories. At Poitiers in 1356 the French king, Jean II ('the Good'), was captured. Three years later, the *Treaty of Brétigny* offered Edward III one-third of France if he gave up his claims to the throne.

The tables are turned

Peace did not last. When Henry V came to the throne of England, he led his army back across the Channel and was victorious. In 1420 the *Treaty of Troyes* made him heir to the French throne but within two years he was dead. French fortunes now began to turn. Their knights were inspired by a peasant girl called Joan of Arc. She claimed that voices of the saints had called her to free her homeland. The English accused her of witchcraft and burned her alive in 1431. However by 1453 France had regained most of the English-occupied lands.

"Dear Kate"

In Shakespeare's play *Henry V*, she is called 'dear Kate'. 'Kate' was Catherine de Valois, daughter of Charles VI of France. In 1420 she married Henry V of England, at the height of his success, but her husband became sick while away at the wars and died in 1422. Nine years later, Catherine secretly married a handsome young Welsh courtier. His name was Owain Tudur or Tudor, and it was their grandson, Henry VII, who founded the most famous dynasty in English history.

Catherine de Valois married Henry V at Troyes. She was crowned Queen of England and gave birth to a son, the future Henry VI, in 1421. Her eldest son by Owain Tudor was Edmund, Earl of Richmond, and he was father to Henry VII, the first Tudor monarch.

✣ 1296
The Welsh Revolt under Madog ap Llywelyn

✣ 1316
Llywelyn Bren revolts in South Wales

✣ 1369
Owain Lawgoch gains support in France

✣ 1400
Owain Glyndŵr rises against English rule

✣ 1403
Welsh and English rebels defeated at Shrewsbury

THE WELSH RISE UP

WALES was changing under English rule. Towns had already been developing in the days of the Welsh princes. Now, new shire or county towns controlled all local trade, and they prospered. In the Welsh heartlands, the new towns took the form of colonies, settled by incomers from England, France or Flanders. Welsh citizens were often forcibly removed to other settlements.

Harlech Castle, completed by King Edward I of England in 1289, was besieged and captured by Owain Glyndŵr's rebels in the spring of 1404. It remained in Welsh hands until 1409.

TROUBLED TIMES

Many Welsh people protested against the taxes and laws brought in by the English. An uprising began in 1294, led by Madog ap Llywelyn, but it was put down in 1295. In 1317 there was a revolt in South Wales, led by Llywelyn Bren. Perhaps the greatest danger to English rule came from Owain Lawgoch, grandson of Llywelyn Fawr. He fought as a mercenary for the French, who called him Yvain de Galles. He planned to reconquer Wales with French help, but was murdered by a secret agent in 1378.

Love and life in fourteenth century Wales is described in the poems of Dafydd ap Gwilym.

POET OF LOVE AND NATURE

Dafydd ap Gwilym is believed by many to be the greatest ever writer in the Welsh language. He was born in the parish of Llanbadarn Fawr, near Aberystwyth, and wrote his masterpieces between 1320 and 1370. He broke with traditional Welsh verse forms and was influenced by French literature. Dafydd wrote light-hearted and joyful poems, many of them about his sweethearts, Morfudd and Dyddgu. He wrote about nature, too, describing the grace of a seagull's flight in a way that still seems very modern today.

A spark catches fire

In 1400 Lord Grey of Ruthin, a personal friend of the English king, Henry IV, siezed some land from his neighbour in the Marches of northeast Wales. Owain Glyndŵr was a middle-aged Welsh nobleman of royal descent. He appealed to the English parliament for justice, but they reacted with contempt, declaring the Welsh to be 'barefoot rascals'. A simple land dispute rapidly became a full-scale national uprising. Owain was supported by all ranks of Welsh society, including monks and bishops. Welsh labourers and students hurried back from England to join him.

Owain Glyndŵr had studied law in London and fought with the English army, but he now became leader of a Welsh uprising. He summoned Welsh parliaments at Machynlleth and Dolgellau.

The longbow was a deadly weapon in the hands of Welsh archers.

Thirteen years of war

Owain was declared Prince of Wales and by 1401 most of his country had joined the uprising. Castles were captured and towns were sacked. Owain joined forces with rebel English barons Henry Percy ('Hotspur') and Edmund Mortimer, but they were defeated at Shrewsbury in 1403. Owain was also supported by the Scots and the French, who sent troops to support him. By 1408, the English were regaining control, but resistance continued until 1413.

MASTERS OF THE LONGBOW

Welsh archers are said to have been the first to develop the longbow. Unlike the shorter Norman bow, it was the full height of a man. It was normally made of yew and had a pull of about 40 kilograms. Arrows were about 78 cm long, made of ash with long metal tips. Goose-feather flights made them spin as they flew through the air. They could even pierce armour. The English used companies of Welsh archers to devastating effect during the Hundred Years' War with France.

✤ **1399**
Henry IV, son of John of Gaunt, is first Lancastrian king

✤ **1453**
Henry VI suffers from mental illness

✤ **1454**
Richard, Duke of York appointed Protector

✤ **1455**
Battle of St Albans. Wars of the Roses begin

✤ **1461**
Edward of York is proclaimed King of England

WARS OF THE ROSES

As battle-hardened soldiers returned from the French wars, many entered the service of powerful English lords. Their job was to bully peasants for payment of taxes, or to fight in private armies. There was no shortage of work for them. For thirty years, from 1455 until 1485, there were civil wars as rival branches of the royal family fought for the throne of England.

A red rose stood for the House of Lancaster. A white rose was the badge of the House of York. When Henry VII came to the throne, he combined both designs in a red-and-white 'Tudor rose'.

Lancaster

York

ENGLISH KINGS

House of Lancaster

✤ Henry IV	1399–1413
✤ Henry V	1413–1422
✤ Henry VI	1422–1461 & 1470–1471

House of York

✤ Edward IV	1461–1470 & 1471–1483
✤ Edward V	1483
✤ Richard III	1483–1485

House of Tudor

✤ Henry VII	1485–150

LANCASTER AND YORK

The Houses of Lancaster and York were both descended from Edward III. Their rivalry came to a head when a Lancastrian king, Henry VI, became too mentally ill to rule. In 1454 Richard, Duke of York, was appointed Protector. When Henry VI got better, Richard would not give up his new-found power, and went to war. Henry VI was defeated at St Albans in 1455, but then Richard was killed at Wakefield in 1460.

There was a great battle at Barnet, to the north of London, on 14 April 1471. Edward IV regained the throne and killed his former ally, Warwick 'the Kingmaker'.

Warwick 'the kingmaker'

The most powerful man in England at this time was not the weak king, but Richard Neville, Earl of Warwick. It was he who had Richard's son proclaimed Edward IV in 1461, the first Yorkist king. Henry VI was imprisoned and exiled. Later, Warwick fell out with Edward and brought Henry VI back to the throne. No wonder he was remembered in history as the 'kingmaker'. Edward returned to seek revenge. Warwick was killed in battle and Henry was murdered in the Tower of London in 1471.

WHO MURDERED THE PRINCES?

Did Richard III murder the princes in the Tower? He had every reason to. Skeletons were found in the Tower in 1674 and buried in Westminster Abbey. However some historians believe that Richard III was not such a villain as he is often made out to be. Might Henry VII have been the true murderer?

THE AGE OF PRINTING

In 1471 an Englishman called William Caxton travelled to the German city of Cologne. There he learned about a new technology, which had been invented in China and developed in Germany and the Netherlands. It was called printing, and it would change the world. Caxton set up his own printing press at Westminster in 1476 and produced about 100 titles.

The march to Bosworth

Edward IV died in 1483. His heir, Edward V, was too young to rule for himself, so he and his young brother were left in the care of their uncle, Richard of Gloucester. They went to live in the Tower of London, but mysteriously, were never seen again. Gloucester was crowned Richard III in the same year, at the request of parliament. He did not rule for long. In 1485 the Earl of Richmond, a Lancastrian, landed in Wales. His name was Henry Tudor and he defeated and killed Richard III at the battle of Bosworth, near Leicester. Henry VII married Elizabeth of York, and brought peace and prosperity to England.

THE MEDIEVAL CASTLE

Castles were built with rings of defences and were hard to attack. They were garrisoned by footsoldiers, archers and men-at-arms.

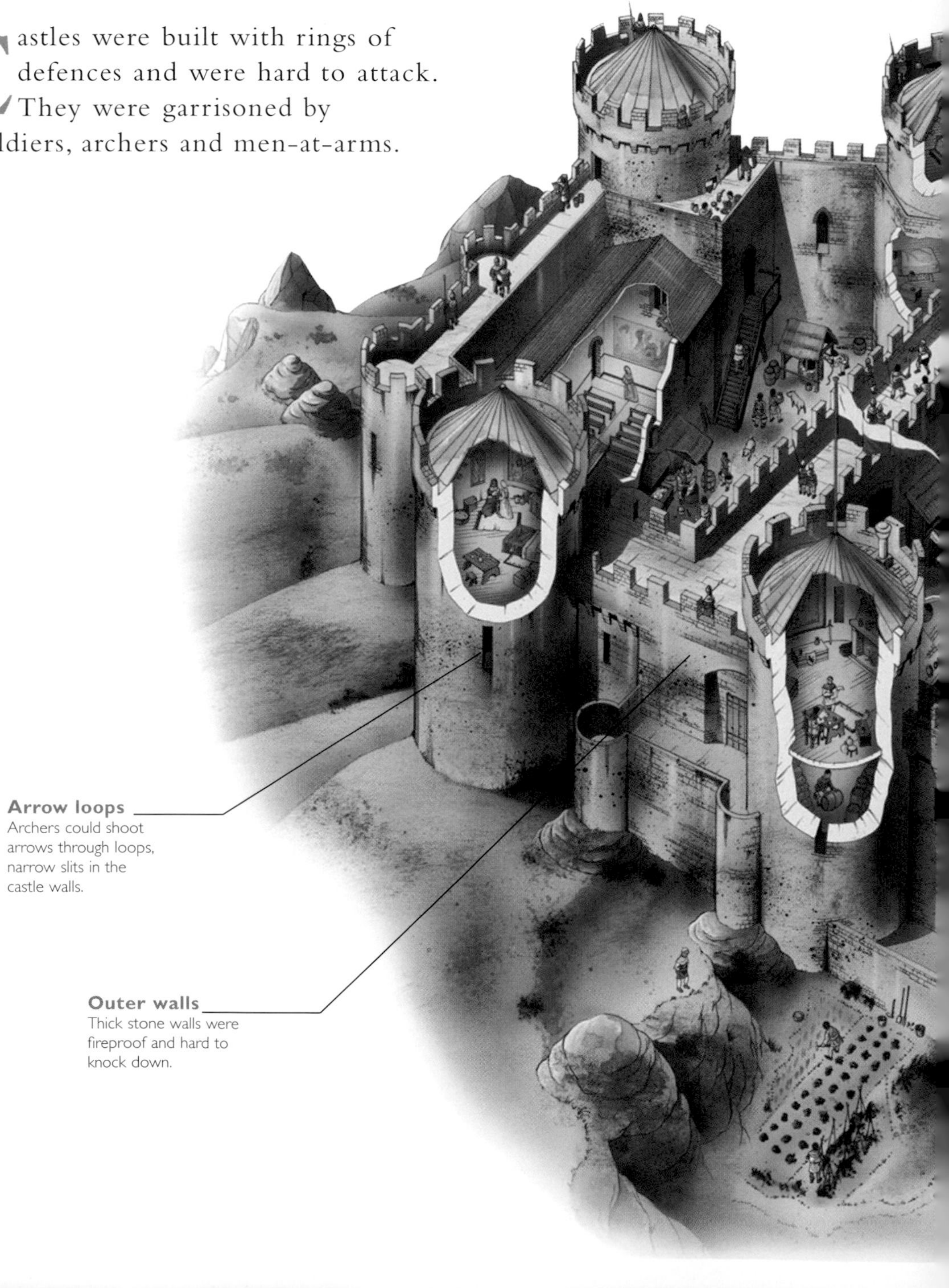

Arrow loops
Archers could shoot arrows through loops, narrow slits in the castle walls.

Outer walls
Thick stone walls were fireproof and hard to knock down.

Battlements
The walls were topped by battlements. These walk-ways were defended by stone blocks called merlons and firing gaps called crenels.
Machicolations
Chutes overhung the outer walls, for dropping missiles on the enemy.
Gatehouse
A strong gate called a portcullis could be dropped to seal off the entrance to the castle.

INDEX

Look up subjects to be found in this book. Illustrations are shown in *italic* print.

A

Aberdyfi 29
Abernethy 12
Acre 20, 21
aircraft 19
Alexander I 30
Alexander II 30
Alexander III 30
Angevin empire 18, *18*, 19
apprentices 35
archery 10, *10*, 38, *38*, 41, *41*
architecture 24, 25, 26, 34, *34-35*
armour 10, 11, *11*, *12-13*, 25, *38-39*, *42-43*
Austria 20

B

Bacon, Roger 19
Ball, John 37
Balliol, Edward 30
Balliol, John 30
banks 35
Bayeux tapestry *11*
Beaumaris castle 25
Becket, Thomas *16*, 17
Bede (Baeda) 26
Bible, the 26, 27
Black Death 36, *36*
Bleddyn ap Cynfyn 29
Bodiam castle *25*
Bosworth, Battle of 43
Breac Maedhóc 32
Brehon Law 32
Brittany 18, 19
Butler, Piers *33*
Burgundy 39

C

Cambridge 19
Canterbury *16*, 17, 26, 27
Canterbury Tales 27, *27*
Cardigan 28
Cashel, Rock of *33*
Castillon, Battle of 39
castles 12, 13, 28, 29, 36, *44-45*
cathedrals 26, *26*, 27, *28*, *33*,
Catherine de Valois 38, *38*
Caxton, William 43
Channel Islands 12
Charles III of France 10
Chaucer, Geoffrey 27
chivalry 22
Cilmeri 29, *29*
clans, Scottish 31
clocks 19
coal 29
Comyn, John 31
Conwy castle *29*
Cornish language 18
costume *12*, *32*
Crécy, Battle of 38
Crusades 19, 20, 21, *21*

D

Dafydd ap Gwilym 40
Dafydd ap Llywelyn 29
Dafydd ap Owain Gwynedd 29
David I 30, *30*
David II 30
d'Avranches, Hugh 13
de Clare, Richard Fitzgilbert 12, *12*, 13, 33
de Londres, Maurice 13
de Montfort, Simon 17
Deheubarth 13, 28
Dermot MacMurrough 12, 13
disease 36, 37, *37*
Domesday Book 11, *11*, 14
Donald III Bán 13, 30
Dublin 26, 32, 33
Dunbar, Battle of 30
Durham *26*

E

Edgar of Scotland 30
Edinburgh *24*
Edmund, Earl of Richmond 39
Edward the Black Prince 38, *38*
Edward Bruce 32, 33
Edward I 18, 20, 29, 30, 40
Edward II 18, 19
Edward III 18, 23, 38, 39
Edward IV 42, 43
Edward V 42, 43
eisteddfodau 28
Eleanor of Aquitaine 18, 19, *19*
Elizabeth of York 43
English language 18, 19, 32

F

famine 36
fashion *12*
Faughart, Battle of 33
feudal system 14, 15
Fitzgerald, Lady Margaret *33*
Fitzosbern, William 13
food 19, *19*, 36
forts 24
France 10, 38, 39
Francis of Assisi 27
French language 18, 19
friars 27, *27*

G

Gaelic language 18
Gaels 32
galloglass 33
Gerald of Wales 28, 29
Germany 35
Giselle 10
Godwin, Earl 10
Grey of Ruthin, Lord 41
Gruffudd ap Cynan 29
Gruffudd ap Llywelyn 28, 29
gunpowder 19, 25
Gwenllian 13, *13*

H

Hadrian IV, Pope 26
Hanseatic League 35
Harald III of Norway 10, 11
Harlech castle *40*
Harold II 10, 11
Hastings, Battle of 10, 11, *11*
Henry I 10, 13, *14*, 16
Henry II 17, 18, 19, 28, 33
Henry III 17, 18
Henry IV 42, 43
Henry V 38, 39, 42
Henry VI 39, 42, 43
Henry VII 39, 42, 43
Henry V, Emperor 16
Henry VI, Emperor 20
heraldry 22
Hereward the Wake 11
Holy Land (Southwest Asia) 20, *20*, 21
hospitals *37*
Hundred Years' War 38, 39, 41

I

Islam 20, 21

J

James III of Scotland 23
Jean II of France 39
Jerusalem 20, 21
Jews 20
Joan of Arc (Jeanne d'Arc) 39
John, King 17, *17*, 18, 19, 32, 33
John of Gaunt 37
Julian of Norwich 27

K

kerns 33
Kidwelly castle 13
Kilkenny *33*
Kilkenny, Statutes of 32, 33
knights *13*, 20, 21, *21*, 22, *22*, 23, *23*, *24*, *38*, *38-39*, *42-43*

L

Lancastrians 42, 43
Largs, battle of 30
Latin language 18, 26, 28
law 16, 17, 32, 37
Leeds 34
Leopold, Duke of Austria 20
lepers 36, *36*
Lewes 17
Lincoln *34*
Liverpool 34
Llanfaes 28
Llywelyn ap Gruffudd 29, *29*
Llywelyn Bren 40
Llywelyn Fawr 29, *29*, 40
London 11, *11*, 34, 35, *35*
London Bridge 35, *35*
Lords of the Isles 31
Louis VII of France 19
Luttrell Psalter 15

M

Madog ap Maredudd 28
Magna Carta 17, *17*
Malcolm III Canmore 12
Malcolm IV 30
Marcher Lords 12, 13, 28
Margaret, Maid of Norway 30
Matilda 16, *16*
medicine 36, 37
Melrose Abbey 26
mining 29
Montgomery, Roger 13
Moors 20
Mortimer, Edmund 41
Muhammad 20

N

Newcastle upon Tyne 34
Normans 10, *10*, 11, *11*, 12, 13, *12-13*, 14, 15, 22, 24, 26, 28, 30, 32, 33
Northmen *see Vikings*
nursing *37*

O

O'Connor, Rory 32
Orders of knights 21, 22, 23
Outremer 20
Owain Glyndwr 40, 41, *41*
Owain Gwynedd 28, 29
Owain Lawgoch 40
Oxford *16*, 19

P

Pale, the 32, *32*, 33
Parliament, English 17, 41
Parliaments, Welsh 29, 41
Peasants' Revolt 37, *37*
Percy, Heny 'Hotspur' 41
Philippe II of France 20
Piers Plowman 27
pilgrimage 27, *27*
plague 36, *36*, 37, *37*
Plantagenet dynasty 18, 19
poets 40
Poitiers, Battle of 38, 39
population 14, 35
Portsmouth 34
printing 13, *13*

R

Rhuddlan, Statute of 29
Rhys ap Gruffudd, the Lord 28, *28*
Rhys ap Tewdwr 13
Richard I 18, 20, *20*, 21
Richard II 18, 33
Richard III 42, 43
Roman Catholic Church 17, 20, 21, 26, 27
Romans 20
Runnymede *17*

S

Saints are listed under their personal names
St Albans, Battle of 42
St David's 27, *28*
Salah-ed-din Yussuf (Saladin) 21
Saracens 21, *21*
Shrewsbury, Battle of 40, 41
Sicily 10
siege warfare 25
Siwan (Joan) 29
Sluys, Battle of 38
Spain 20
spectacles 19
spinning wheels 15
sports *34*, 35
stained glass *12*, 26, *26*
Stephen 10, 16, 18, 28
Stewart/Stuart dynasty 31
Stirling Bridge, Battle of 31, *31*
Srata Florida (Ystrad Fflur) 28

T

taxes 37, 42
Thames, River 11,
theatre 27
Tinchebrai, battle of 16
tithes 15
Tostig 10, 11
tournaments 22, *22*, 23, *23*
Tower of London 11, *11*, 34, 37, 43
trade 33, 35
Trahaearn ap Caradog 29
Troyes, Treaty of 39
Tudor, Owain 39
Tudor dynasty 39, 42, 43
Tyler, Wat 37

U

universities 19
Urban II, Pope 20

V

Vikings 10
villeins 14, 15

W

Wakefield, Battle of 42
Wallace, William 31
Wars of the Roses 42, 43, *42-43*
weapons 10, *10*, 12-13, 21, *21*, 23, 25, 38, *38*, 41, *41*, 42-43,
Welsh language 18
Wessex, Kingdom of 10
Westminster Abbey 27
William I of England 10, 11, 12, 13
William II of England 11, 13, 16
William the Lion 30
windmills 14
Windsor, Treaty of 32
Witan, the 10
witchcraft 39
Wycliffe, John 27

Y

York 26
Yorkists 42, 43

Z

zoos 34

ACKNOWLEDGEMENTS

The publishers would like to thank the following sources for the use of their images:

Page 11 (B/R) Pavel Libera/Corbis; 16 (T/R) Leonard de Selva/Corbis; 26 (T/R) Archivo Iconografico/Corbis; 27 (B/L) Mary Evans Picture Library; 28 (B) Adam Woolfitt/Corbis; 31 (B/R) Bob Krist/Corbis; 34 (T/L) Lincolnshire County Council; 35 (T/R) Bridgeman Art Library; 37 (B/L) Bettmann/Corbis; 40 (T/R) Dean Conger/Corbis

All other photographs from MKP Archives

The publishers would like to thank the artists whose work appears in this book:

Julie Banyard, Richard Berridge/SpecsArt, Vanessa Card, Nicholas Forder, Peter Gregory, Alan Hancocks, Sally Holmes, Richard Hook/Linden Artists, Janos Marffy, Angus McBride/LindenArtists, Terry Riley, Martin Sanders, Peter Sarson, Rob Sheffield, Guy Smith/Mainline, Studio Galante, Rudi Vizi, Mike White/Temple Rogers